El Camino de Santiago

A 1st Hand View of Walking 220 kms in

9 Days Across the North of Spain

Independently Published

Revision 3.0

ASIN: B00KRBTV2A

ISBN: 9781980450931

Copyright © Simon Green 2024.

"By failing to prepare,

you are preparing to fail."

Benjamin Franklin

Thanks and Dedications

Thank you to every person we met along the way, you all helped to make this experience a positive one.

If you are reading this book, many thanks to you for choosing it, I hope that you find it both interesting and useful. ....

Contents

About The Book

El Camino de Santiago: A 1st Hand View of Walking 220 kms in 9 Days Across the North of Spain

Do you want to learn more about El Camino De Santiago (or The Way of St James) from real first-hand experience?

Described in this book you will find lots of practical information that will help you better plan and prepare for walking El Camino de Santiago. Also included is the journal written during the experience documenting each of the nine days, itself containing valuable information.

Newly added is a fully updated chapter revealing the types of people you will likely come across on your journey, all derived from official data.

By reading this book you will experience what it is like to walk 220kms to Santiago de Compostela in 9 days and feel better prepared for one of the most challenging and rewarding experiences of your life, thanks for reading!

A Brief History of El Camino de Santiago

El Camino de Santiago (or in English, "The Way of St. James") was one of the most important Christian pilgrimages during the Middle Ages, together with those leading to Rome and Jerusalem. The name "El Camino de Santiago" is given to any of the pilgrim routes that end at the shrine of the apostle St. James in the Cathedral of Santiago de Compostela, in Galicia in the north-west of Spain. The location of the shrine is where it is believed the remains of the saint were buried.

Originally, El Camino de Santiago was one of dozens of original pilgrim routes to Santiago de Compostela; however, only a few of these are still active routes today. Traditionally, as with most pilgrimages, El Camino began from your home, in whatever city or country that may be, and then ended at the pilgrimage destination.

By the 1980s, only a few pilgrims per year arrived in Santiago de Compostela, but later the route started to attract a growing number of 'modern-day' pilgrims from around the globe. In October 1987, the Way was declared the first 'European Cultural Route' by the Council of Europe, and in 2015 it was designated a UNESCO World Heritage Site.

The most famous Camino route is 'El Camino Francés' (The French Way) officially starting in St. Jean Pied de Port in the French Pyrenees. This route is approximately 800 kms long and would take around five weeks to complete at a steady pace.

The main symbol of El Camino de Santiago is the scallop shell which can often be found on the shores of Galicia. The scallop shell also acts as a visual metaphor in that the grooves in the shell represent the various routes that pilgrims travel to Santiago and that they all eventually arrive at a single destination.

Although many people choose to do El Camino de Santiago for religious or spiritual reasons, this isn't the same for all. Some want to take part in the adventure, potentially in a foreign country, for the challenge of simple living and walking for days or weeks on end in the countryside.

By the end of the journey, many do end up considering the experience to have been a spiritual one. And somewhat a 'retreat', as you are able to remove yourself from the typical stresses and routines of modern-day life. You will have a lot of time to be alone with yourself, and thanks to that time, you will find that you are able to think and consider things more clearly. For this reason, some people do find a kind of spirituality resulting from the overall experience.

The 25th of July is officially the 'Day of St. James' and is a religious holiday in Santiago de Compostela and Galicia. If the 25th of July falls on a Sunday, then this is considered a Holy Year.

Despite being a Monday, the 25th of July of 2016 was exceptional as Pope Francis declared it to be a 'Holy Year of Mercy' or an 'Extraordinary Jubilee of Mercy', so was an important year for many religious pilgrims.

The number of pilgrims travelling on El Camino de Santiago is increasing year after year, 277,854 pilgrims registered in Santiago in 2016, compared to 347,578 (a 25% increase) by the end of 2019. In the next chapter, I include more statistics about the kinds of people you are likely to meet.

The People on El Camino de Santiago

As part of all excellent adventures, it is interesting to meet people from around the world, and El Camino de Santiago provides plenty of opportunities to do just that.

One thing to be aware of is that the people you meet in the first albergue (and there can be up to 50 people sleeping in one room!), you will probably be seeing a lot of them over the next few days. As everyone is walking towards the same destination, with some exceptions, everyone generally stops off in the same village for lunch and then later in the same town at the end of the day.

Below I provide some charts and statistics about the 'typical' people you will find walking El Camino together with you. All data has been taken from the website of the official Pilgrim's Reception Office (la

Oficina del Peregrino) in Santiago for the last five complete years (2014-2019).

Male / Female split

The split between the number of male and female pilgrims remains fairly even throughout the years. Combined, you can see the steady increase in overall people.

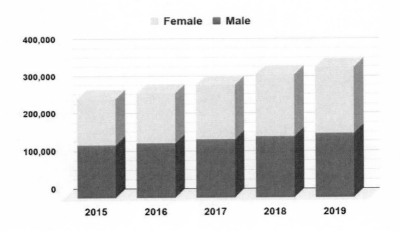

Age Ranges

There is no minimum or maximum age for walking El Camino. The main requirement is that you are physically (and mentally) prepared for the enduring days of walking kilometres/miles until you reach the goal. That said, the youngest person I saw was a three-year-old, being carried along very carefully and responsibly by the parents in a rucksack-style baby harness.

The below chart shows five groups (one for each year 2014-2019) and groups of three age-ranges ('Less Than 30', 'Between 30–60', and 'Over 60'), again you can see the regular steady increase in numbers.

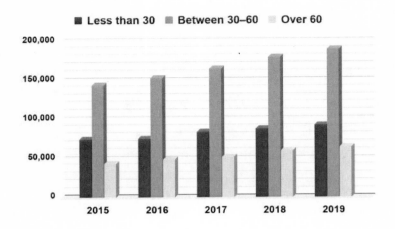

Age ranges

"Top 10" Nationalities

The below chart shows the ten most common nationalities of the people that walked or cycled El Camino between 2014 and 2019.

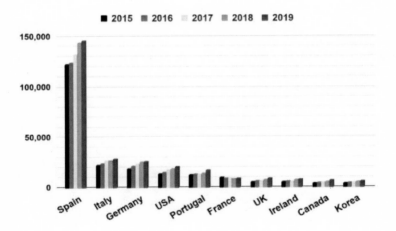

People's Motivation

We travel along El Camino for a variety of different reasons. On completion and arrival to the Pilgrim's Office in Santiago, you are asked to provide your reason for completing the journey, choosing from one of the three following answers, 'Religious & Other', 'Religious', and 'Non-Religious', this is how the people responded.

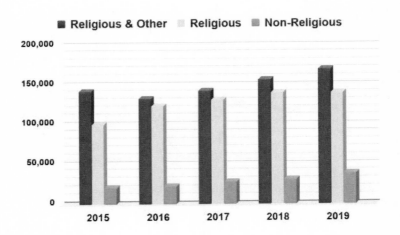

The Most Popular Months of the Year

If you are planning to travel El Camino in the future, this following chart may be of interest as taking data from the last five years you can see the most popular (i.e. busiest) times of the year for people taking part.

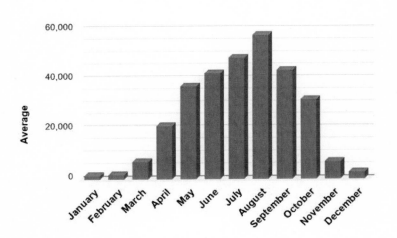

My Motivation

The first time I heard about 'El Camino de Santiago' (or 'The Way of St. James'), was perhaps several years before I set out to walk it. Likely it would have been while I was reading one of the various books I had that described living in and travelling around Spain. I would have read about this 'pilgrimage' that is over two-thousand years old (and that still exists today), about the adventures and of the experiences that people have had, shared and endured on these various routes to Santiago de Compostela. That would have been enough to draw me in.

My reasons for doing it were purely for the adventure, the experience and the challenge. The adventure; travelling to and through somewhere I've never been before. For the experiences, everything from feelings of relaxation to complete exhaustion, being able to walk for days through the Spanish countryside, in all weathers, while appreciating my environment and situation. The incredible views and of course the people that would flavour my journey and the change of pace and lifestyle for a few days. Finally, the challenge of starting in one location, and walking to our destination over 220kms (137 miles) away in just nine days while carrying all of our own belongings.

I walked this route with my girlfriend. We are both active people, and we enjoy travelling, so when I explained I wanted to walk part of El Camino de Santiago thankfully she was also enthusiastic about it and wanted to do it.

Of course, the actual walking to Santiago is only part of the overall challenge, the training and preparations beforehand also count.

As we were planning to be reasonably self-sufficient during the whole journey, we needed to be responsible for the planning and logistics of being in the right place at the right time, also on choosing the right equipment to take with us, and what to leave behind. All of this is better when you can share the responsibility and motivate each other. So the challenge had been set!

Prequel to Day One

To arrive at our starting point, the city of Ponferrada in the north-west of Spain, we initially started our journey from Barcelona, where we were living.

In the early part of September, we flew to the city of Santander (population of 172,000) and stayed in the beautiful region of Asturias for a couple of days. Afterwards, we caught a bus to Ponferrada, a fairly small city with a population of 65,000. On arrival, we walked for about twenty minutes to Ponferrada's city centre to find some accommodation for the night. We hadn't booked anything in advance, but we easily found a private hostel (or 'Albergue' as they are known in Spanish) and quickly checked in. We left our modest belongings in the room and set off to have a look around the city.

It wasn't long until we found the impressive twelfth-century Templar Castle. Unfortunately, it was late in the afternoon and we didn't have enough time to enter and have a look around, so instead we had to sit back and admire its grandness from the outside.

Later we found the main square where we were able to sit down and enjoy an evening meal and talk about our expectations for the next day and of those that lay ahead. We were full of anticipation, like when you know something exciting is about to happen, but you're not exactly sure of the outcome.

We had dedicated nine days to walking El Camino, which may work out to be about the average most people choose. Seeing our pre-planned journey on the map seemed slightly pathetic at first, especially when compared to the entire route, which is 790 km (500 miles) and that could take a month or more to complete. Still, within these nine days, we were planning to walk over 220 kms (137 miles), with no scheduled rest days, and carrying rucksacks weighing around 8kg. We knew it would be a great challenge and adventure, and we were both excited about getting started.

The pages ahead include the day-to-day journal I wrote during the journey. I hope it gives you a good idea about the experience.

¡Bon Camino!

Day One:

Ponferrada to Villafranca del Bierzo

Distance to Santiago: **220kms**

Stage Length: **24kms**

The Templar Castle of Ponferrada.

The alarm sounded at 07:00, we woke up and were out of bed without any problem. The first day of our

El Camino de Santiago is finally here. We got ready, re-packed our partly unpacked bags and left the albergue (the typical hostel used by pilgrims travelling on El Camino) at 07:50. It is dark, and it's raining. We are in Ponferrada, a city that is over 220kms from our destination of Santiago de Compostela. We set off eagerly through the dark, wet streets that lead us out of the city, following a route that we had established the previous day. We walk over the ancient stone bridge, past the Templar Castle and we soon find ourselves on the lower outskirts of the city. It is very quiet. At about 08:30 in the morning and after having climbed out of the valley of Ponferrada, we look back and see the city in the distance, now illuminated in daylight. It is still raining, the clouds are low and heavy and they give no indication that the rain is going to stop anytime soon. We gracefully slide through the countryside. Kilometre after kilometre, the small villages we walk through seem to appear and then drift off behind us as we continue on our journey.

The plan was to stop in the village Cacabelos for lunch, but we arrived at 11:45, much earlier than expected. Still, we buy lunch from a small bakery with the intention of stopping to eat it later in the day. We pack the food in our bags and continue walking out of Cacabelos. It's still raining.

By about 13:00 we find ourselves once again immersed in the middle of the countryside. Looking out in all directions, we see acre after acre of vineyards which stretch out almost as far as the eye can see. We stop for a moment in the rain, to take in this spectacular scene. The only sound we can hear is of the falling rain landing on the plants all around us. Occasionally we come across people but it is certainly not busy. It has now been about five hours of continuous walking since we set off this morning and we're starting to feel pretty hungry, but there is nowhere for us to stop and take cover from the rain so we can eat, so we have no choice but to keep moving.

We finally arrive to the albergue of Villafranca del Bierzo at 14:45 and check-in easily. After almost seven hours of walking without a proper rest nor having eaten lunch we are feeling pretty exhausted. We pay 8€ each to the girl at the entrance which covers the accommodation for the night and as a 'bonus' it also includes a "hot hydro-massage shower", it was an easy sell. We're tired and hungry, so after preparing our beds we sit outside the albergue and finally get to eat our lunch, stretch our legs and relax a little. By this time the rain has stopped, and the sun makes a welcome appearance from behind the clouds!

We leave the albergue to go and have a look around the village. We see various styles of churches and buildings built during different eras, and walking around you can sense the deep history this place has developed throughout the past centuries. Looking further out into the distance, we see that the whole village is surrounded by mountains which provides incredible views in all directions.

It's beginning to turn chilly now, and a cold wind is starting to pick up. We get the impression this place would be bitterly cold during the wintertime, and due to its remote location, it appears fairly cut off from other towns in the area. I imagine the locals are hardened individuals with interesting stories to tell from throughout the years.

We find a welcoming restaurant in one of the main plazas of the village and sit down to eat an extremely good three-course meal with a bottle of red wine. I notice that whilst eating, all the colours of my surroundings slowly start to fade back to normal and become more vibrant, for sure it's the energy returning to me. The joy of good food!

We're feeling tired now, partly due to not having slept much last night in Ponferrada. We have another early start scheduled for the morning, so our plan for the rest of the evening is to head back to the albergue and be in bed early and asleep by 21:00. Day One: complete!

Day Two:

Villafranca del Bierzo to O Cebreiro

Distance to Santiago: **191 kms**

Stage Length: **28.5 kms**

Foggy Start.

This morning we left the albergue at 07:15 and again like yesterday we started the walk in darkness. We're following the road out of Villafranca del Bierzo, but unlike yesterday, when we were on tranquil countryside trails, today we'll be walking mainly on asphalt roads.

It will also be one of the longest stages at over 28 kms and apparently one of the toughest of the whole Camino due to the final 8kms being all uphill.

After some kilometres of steady walking, our legs start to feel warmed up and we're going strong again. Thankfully, after yesterday's walk we were not feeling as stiff as expected, and as a bonus the weather had improved with no rain forecast for the day, instead we have white clouds, blue skies and sun.

By 09:00 we had already walked about 8km, and having not eaten breakfast yet, we see a sign advertising 'BIG COFFEE AND TOAST'. This is something we just cannot resist, so we stop for a while to sit down at a table in the small café and enjoy our breakfast.

The plan was to stop and eat lunch just before the final 8km climb, in a place called 'Hospital', but again we arrived much earlier than expected, so we decided to keep going. After several kilometres of walking uphill on the road, the marked route takes a sharp drop and a left turn onto a gravel path leading through a forest, after all that uphill effort! As expected, the downhill doesn't last for long and we soon start heading upwards again. Carefully winding our way up through the trees, we pass a couple from Germany, who with their three-year-old daughter have stopped to take advantage of the shade and eat their lunch. It has been a hot day today, and the trees provide a welcome break from being in the sun.

After an hour or so of walking up through the forest, the trail leads us out through an opening in the trees. Exiting the forest we find ourselves walking along a singletrack path on the side of a hill. Out to our left, there is a very deep valley below us, and we have incredible views of several mountain ranges in the distance. Now fully out of the trees we can see, for the first time in several hours the elevation gain we've made, and it is impressive.

Walking up this desolate mountain path, we feel like we are so far away from civilisation. The trail takes us more inland and we do eventually pass some remote farmhouses and their out-buildings that overlook acres upon acres of farmland.

After several kilometres more we pass an albergue run by a family of cattle farmers, but the one we are looking for is a further 2kms up on the top of the mountain, so we keep on walking. The amazing views we have to the left of us, of the distant green mountains and the rich blue sky, helps us to take our minds off our aching legs and focus on the last couple of kilometres that lie ahead. That and the curiosity of badly wanting to see the whole view from the top of this mountain, which we were steadily approaching.

We eventually arrive at our destination, 'O Cebreiro' with its wider population of about 1,200, it offers a breath-taking 360 degree view. We're hot, sweaty and tired, but we easily find our way to the building that will be our accommodation for the night. It is a modern building and being perched on the peak of a mountain it feels very isolated. Once again it is becoming a bit cold now and being so remote and exposed, I get the feeling it's going to be a cold night.

Once successfully checked in to the albergue, we find our beds and get cleaned up. The bedroom is large, open planned and has about twenty-five to thirty bunk beds, about half are currently occupied either with bags or their owners for the night. We have a nap ourselves and rest for an hour. Later we get up and go out to have a look around the village.

It doesn't take long to find our way around as there are just a few stone buildings each housing either a church, restaurants, gift shops or houses. We find a low wall to take a seat on at the perimeter of the village, and we have time to take in the stunning views that we have surrounding us. We sit and contemplate our journey up to now and what awaits us during the days that lay ahead.

The sun is now fairly low in the sky and casting long drawn-out shadows all over the valley below us. There are several other people, all 'pilgrims' like ourselves, who are also sitting or standing around. We all stare out in silence, taking in this special moment of the day.

We go for dinner at one of the few restaurants in the village and we eat like kings for just 9€ each, devouring every last morsel of our three course meal. We are once again in bed early at 21:00.

Day Three:

Cebreiro to Triacastela

Distance to Santiago: **162kms**

Stage Length: **21kms**

Bea and a Camino Cow.

Our sleep is disturbed several times during the night, no thanks to a few of the fifty-plus people we are sharing the room with who are heavy snorers, but we get out of bed as planned at 06:30.

Once dressed, I open the main door of the albergue to have a look outside; it's dark, wet and very foggy. Given our altitude of 1,330m, we seem to be in the middle of a dense cloud, and I can see no further than a few meters in front of me.

We quietly pack the rest of our things and leave the albergue. Stepping carefully outside into the cloud, we slowly make our way around the outside of the albergue to find the asphalt road and begin our descent off the mountain. Thankfully our torches light up the route ahead and help make the job much easier. It's a nice walk to the bottom of the valley, which lasts for about an hour and for the most part we are walking through this thick fog. It's still quite dark, and there's a full moon above which casts a certain eeriness over everything. Later we only need to use our torches when the occasional car passes to indicate our whereabouts.

After an hour or two daylight arrives. We are now walking through more farmland, all off-road and mainly leading downhill. There was one very steep, muddy uphill section that took a bit of effort to get up but luckily we found an open bar at the top. We stop there for breakfast, ordering coffee, 'big toast' and freshly squeezed orange juice. Half an hour later and refuelled, we set off once again and continued our journey.

It's all downhill for now, and at times we still find ourselves walking through patches of fog which block the view of the valley below. Today is definitely a short one in terms of distance as we arrive at the planned albergue in Triacastela nice and early at 12:30, so today will definitely count as more of a rest day.

We go for a walk around the village – it's quite small, and there's not much to see except for the usual restaurants catering mainly to the pilgrims who pass through. We find a supermarket and take advantage by buying some snacks and food with the intention of cooking it later in the evening.

As it's still reasonably early, we go to a nice looking restaurant and order a three-course lunch. We are now one-third of the way through the walk and we're starting to feel quite stiff with aching muscles in our legs and back. We're stretching regularly, so it's just the body adjusting, getting used to walking so much and carrying the bag of belongings. Tomorrow will be a much shorter day again at just over 18kms so I guess we'll be arriving at our destination of Sarria, all being well at about 12:00.

It's now 16:45 and we head back to the albergue for a shower and a rest. This time our bedroom is much smaller than usual with just two bunk beds, we share the room with two French ladies in their 50s.

We have an afternoon snooze and wake up at about 19:00 then head out for another walk around the village. We're not feeling as hungry as we expected due to the big lunch we ate earlier so we head back to the albergue and we're in bed at 22:00.

Day Four:

Triacastela to Sarria

Distance to Santiago: **136kms**

Stage Length: **18.5kms**

One of the many 'motivational signs' along the way showing "Don't STOP walking".

The two French ladies snored a lot during the night, but surprisingly it has been one of the best night's sleep I've had in a while. Perhaps because we were just four people in one room and not fifty-plus like we've been used to during the two previous nights. We stay in bed a bit longer than usual and get up at 07:00, we don't hang around and we're on the road again by 07:20. Outside it's wet, it's been raining during the night, and it's still drizzling now.

Half an hour later, the rain starts to come down a lot heavier which forces us to stop and put the rain covers on our bags to keep them and our belongings dry. We follow El Camino through more farmland, at times the route is not well marked but luckily we manage to find the correct way without any back-tracking. Up until now, the route has been very well sign-posted and easy to follow thanks to the clear signs and typical yellow arrows or scallop shells that indicate the way of El Camino de Santiago.

Yesterday afternoon in a moment of tiredness, I made the huge mistake of cutting the loose skin off two blisters I had on my right foot. Personal note, I will never, I repeat NEVER do this again. For some reason, I thought the raw skin would have dried up enough by the morning, of course not. It is now very painful to walk on. I treat it as best I can (given our supplies) and try to ignore the pain. I don't know what I was thinking.

A couple of hours into the walk we meet Beni, a forty-nine year old Spanish man who began his walk much further away than us, starting near the Pyrenees. The three of us stop off for a coffee and continue along El Camino, we're looking forward to completing this short stage of 18.5kms. We are walking through more countryside on the way to Sarria, our destination for today. There are so many breath-taking views that should inspire calm and tranquillity, but every step is like I'm walking on fire.

We've met people before now on El Camino, you walk together for a while, chatting, sharing experiences and after some time you bid each other farewell until the next time you meet as everyone is generally walking in the same direction. But this guy Beni seems content in sticking with us and he doesn't seem like he wants to part company. When we stop, he stops, when we continue he comes with us.

Being out in the countryside, in all types of weather is a very refreshing and liberating experience. You have a lot of time to think and contemplate things whilst walking along.

The rain has now stopped. We start to enter the town of Sarria at about 12:00. Beni's plan, he told us earlier, was to continue to the next village beyond Sarria, but he heard from someone along the way that there is an 'octopus festival' happening here, in Sarria sometime soon. During this time, we are explained that all the local bars prepare cooked octopus as their specialty dish and this Beni, apparently loves a bit of octopus, so he decides to hang around and stay here for the night also.

We arrive at a tourist office on the outskirts to ask for directions to some albergues. Here we're also able to get another stamp for our credenciales or 'pilgrim passports'. We enquire about the town's 'octopus festival' and they told us that it's actually next week! I'm thinking "great, with any luck he'll continue to the next town as per his original plan" but no, he's decided to follow us into the town centre where we all find an albergue, and the reception assigns us the same room. We are shown to a room containing four beds. I think that if it's not him it would be with someone else. He seems to be an experienced traveller, he's not threatening in any way but he just doesn't seem to want to be on his own. What can you do, I guess maybe he's just lonely and wants some company.

All three of us go for a walk around Sarria and find a bar serving octopus ahead of the festival and we get well fed. Afterwards we go out to explore the town for an hour or so. It's a nice sunny day now and after a while we sit down at a bar by the river to drink a couple of beers and then return to the albergue. I prepare a big cup of tea made from fresh pine needles that I collected along the way and end up cooking the food that I've been carrying around since the last stop which will also make the bag a bit lighter. We're both now starting to get a bit frustrated with this guy, so we head out for a walk on our own to discuss how we're going to say goodbye to Beni.

Day Five:

Sarria to Portomarín

Distance to Santiago: **114kms**

Stage Length: **22.5kms**

Arriving at the entrance of Portomarín.

We woke up at 06:30 and got ready as usual swiftly leaving the albergue. It had been raining during the night again, the ground was wet but thankfully it has stopped now. Beni also gets ready quickly and leaves with us. Half an hour or so into the walk, we're again in the middle of the countryside with fantastic views, and we see a beautiful sunrise that I'll remember for some time. Beni is friendly enough, but he's outstayed his welcome now. We stop to take some photos; he's still there. Walking slowly doesn't help either. We stop a few times to get the passport stamped and stop for more photos and he still won't leave us. We continue with soft tactics and if we speak in English he disappears, so we continue doing this for a while!

We haven't seen him now for over an hour and up ahead we see over a hundred, very loud and enthusiastic young pilgrims, who turn out partly to be a group of about fifty Portuguese school children getting ready to set off on their first day of El Camino. We get the impression that today is going to be busy. We're hoping that we've lost Beni now as we're sure he's ahead of this group.

On arrival in Santiago de Compostela, you receive a final stamp in your pilgrim's passport to officially confirm your arrival and completion of the journey. You also receive a certificate written in Latin (the Compostela) confirming the start point and end of your journey. You only receive this certificate if you have walked over 100kms and the closest and most convenient point to start from in order to achieve this certificate is Sarria. Sarria also has good bus and rail connections to and from other places in Spain, and is 114kms from Santiago. Thanks to this, as we found out, this is where many people choose to start their walk.

We really start to notice the change of atmosphere now, whereas before the paths we were following were calm and almost tranquil, they have now become a lot busier. During the last few days, we've been seeing the same people as we pass each other on our way to Santiago, but today we start to see a lot of new and fresher faces.

Today we are again walking mainly through farmland. It started off with a few kilometres of uphill trails. After some time we stop off for a coffee at a road-side bar where we watch many of the people we've just passed now over-taking us. There are so many more people out today than what we've been used to. We decide to call ahead to a private albergue in Portomarín and reserve a place to stay for the night. We managed to reserve two beds on the condition that we arrive before 13:00 which is in one hour and forty minutes, and we still have 11kms to walk. We set off and pick up the pace and it shows, we're in a bit of a rush!

We arrived in Portomarín amazingly twenty minutes before the deadline. We cross over the impressive, Roman built stone bridge that spans the river Minho, and ten minutes later, we are checked into the albergue without any problems. They tell us that today is their town's annual festival and there will be big celebrations!

We go and do some food shopping, eat lunch, and on the way back to the albergue, who do we see, but Beni! He says he is going to continue to the next village this time and we don't convince him to do otherwise. We shake hands and part company.

At about 14:00 we are sitting outside the albergue enjoying a cold beer and we hear people setting off fireworks from the car park outside. We're thinking that, if it's like this now, what is it going to be like this evening when we're trying to sleep!

We go back to the albergue to shower, sort out the injury on my foot (!) and have a lie down to rest. We are now over halfway and have four more days of walking until we reach Santiago.

At about 18:00 we head out to see what's happening in the town. They've set up a huge stage in the middle of the main plaza which appears to be ready for a featured music group by the name of 'Orquesta Gran Parada'. We sit down at a restaurant and ordered another pilgrim's set menu. Later we walk around the outskirts and see some beautiful views of the river as the sun is setting. We head back to the albergue once more, and we're in bed by 22:00.

Day Six:

Portomarín to Palas de Rei

Distance to Santiago: **92 kms**

Stage Length: **25 kms**

The Albergue of Palas de Rei.

We leave the albergue of Portomarín at 07:15, and after less than five minutes we see the huge swarm of Portuguese school children walking down the hill and into the forest below, starting their second day. Somehow we manage to pass them all in about thirty minutes, most of them still seem to be half asleep. We're walking along a forest path with a quiet road running on the right-hand side. After a couple of hours we stop off for a mug of coffee and a 'big toast'. Setting off again is painful, due to the damn blisters. Due to this it seems I've started to walk with a bit of a limp and as a result I have this sharp pain in my lower back with every step I take. This lasts for a few hours but I walk it off, thanks to this I don't feel the pain so much in my foot, yay!

These days feel a lot more 'touristy' when compared to the start of our journey. There are so many more people out now, much louder and more energetic than us. There seems to be a constant competition to arrive at the albergue as soon as possible so as to guarantee a bed for the night. It really couldn't be more different to the 'relaxed' atmosphere that we've been used to.

Up until now, we've been following signs indicating the correct way, and they haven't given any indication of remaining distance. Now we've started to see these small stone markers with the typical yellow Camino scallop shell. These markers now show how many kilometres there are left until we reach our destination of Santiago. It's nice and very motivating to see the distance counting down in front of you. We now have 68.4kms of walking until we reach Santiago de Compostela!

We arrive at the albergue at 12:35 and join the queue of people waiting for it to open at 13:00. Once in, we prepare the bed with the supplied liner sheets and head out into the town for some food, a drink and a look around. The albergue is a fairly modern building, nice and clean with two floors. Our room is in the upper half and can accommodate up to forty people.

In general we're starting to feel pretty tired now with the racing around. It really makes us appreciate the times when we could just relax with peace and quiet.

We head into the town of Palas de Rei, which is a very small and quiet place. We don't find much that catches our attention, but we do find a large supermarket where we stock up on some different food for lunch, later for dinner and for breakfast tomorrow morning. We are starting to feel a bit tired of the typical pilgrim set menus, as amazing as they are, change is also a good thing.

Tomorrow will be one of the longest stages of El Camino at 30kms (including the long walk out of town), but apparently, it feels much longer due to the many long hills you need to climb and descend.

Luckily now, the afternoon is warm and sunny, and outside the albergue there is a large grassy area with lots of trees providing shade from the sun and places to prepare barbecues. One of our 'luxury' items we each brought with us was a compact travel hammock, which we planned to make good use of now. We carefully set them up between trees and made some sandwiches for lunch with the food we bought earlier in the town's supermarket. After lunch we take the well earned opportunity to laze around all afternoon, it feels so good swaying in the shade especially as the weather is so nice.

Later we take a short walk down into the town and visit a small church where we receive two more stamps for our pilgrim passports. We have a long journey ahead of us tomorrow so we're planning to get up at 05:30 and out the door by 06:00, so we head back to the albergue to get some more rest.

Day Seven:

Palas de Rei to Arzúa

Distance to Santiago: **68kms**

Stage Length: **30kms**

Passports Stamped Here

We wake up at 05:45 and leave the albergue not long after that. We get the torches out and start the walk by entering a forest, We're moving at a good pace. All the blisters have now healed and are now pain free, just how we like it, now it's just aching legs! I guess after almost two-hundred kilometres walking in seven days, this can be expected.

We collect a few more stamps along the way for our passports. We're starting to see familiar faces along the way again, and occasionally we see people that we thought we passed earlier in the day ahead of us. There's a lot of talk about people catching taxis to the next village, and if not for themselves, sending their bags up ahead using a transport service to help lighten their load. In one way I understand why some people do it, because what we're doing isn't easy. It's not just physically tiring but also mentally, and I wonder about the people doing it, whether it is something they would later regret.

Because of the long stage today, some people have decided to split it into two shorter stages. We're not feeling too bad so we decided to keep going.

It's now 13:30 and we stop off for a quick beer. We've been walking mainly through the countryside again today, through some forests and occasionally along a main road. Today has mainly been a day of getting on with it and watching the kilometres countdown. We haven't noticed much of interest today although the weather has been really nice, warm and sunny again. We're almost there!

We have already walked over 26kms today so we've almost completed the longest day. However we are thinking of changing the plan a little for tomorrow and walking an extra 15kms on top of the 19kms that we have planned, so 34kms in total, which will put us in a place called 'Monte do Gozo'. Monte do Gozo is just 5kms before Santiago which means that when we leave the albergue on the final day, we will arrive in Santiago much earlier in the morning beating the rush. Also, because Monte do Gozo is on top of a large hill overlooking Santiago, it is apparently a great place to see the city from as the sun goes down. If we decide to do this, it will mean a 34km walk (the longest up until now) BUT the following morning, we will have earned a straightforward walk of just 5kms into Santiago, arriving much earlier than usual and resulting in more time to explore the city.

But back to today, we arrived at our destination of Arzúa at about 14:30. The main municipal Albergue was already full, which doesn't surprise us as people generally start queuing up from about 12:30 waiting for it to open.

Arzúa seems to be the biggest town we've seen since we left Ponferrada seven days ago. Following the main street into town, we see various signs indicating where we can find three other privately run albergues. Two signs each indicate 100m away, another shows 20m, so naturally, we follow the sign to the closer one. We enter the door and walk in, the lady on reception says she only has one room with two beds available at 12.50€ each for the night. At first, this seemed quite expensive as prices up until now have been between 5€ to 10€. But we don't hesitate for a second, and we happily hand over the money. She shows us the room and instead of seeing a room filled with over twenty bunk beds we see a small, windowless room with just two single beds. Bliss! And as if that wasn't good enough it also had its own private and lockable bathroom, another little luxury we haven't been used to in the last week or so. In the five minutes it takes us to complete the check-in, four other people have come in also looking for a place to sleep, but each one is being told that this albergue is now full!

We are tired and tomorrow will be tough, but we are still enthusiastic about doing the 34kms to Monte de Gozo. If needed, there is a small village after around 20-25km of walking where we could stop for the night, but if we do manage to complete the 34kms and arrive to Monte do Gozo tomorrow, it would be great for three reasons. 1) Being able to see the kilometres countdown to a remaining 6kms. 2) To see the sunset from the top of Monte de Gozo. And 3) To wake up 'late' on the final morning and enjoy a calm, relaxed walk into Santiago.

Back in the albergue in Arzúa, we get showered and cleaned up. Later we have a walk around the town and buy some food. For some reason I have a lot of pain in both of my feet, to the point where it's causing me to limp again. I am also feeling really tired, and with this pain in my feet and legs I'm a bit worried about the long day we have planned for tomorrow. I decided to go back to the albergue to get some rest and sleep.

Day Eight:

Arzúa to Monte do Gozo

Distance to Santiago: **39kms**

Stage Length: **34kms**

Santiago Approaching

The alarm sounds at 06:30. I've slept well and amazingly, my legs feel much better than expected. I keep thinking about the distance we're going to walk today and how we're going to be feeling in the evening! We set off again at about 07:20 after having enjoyed a nice lie-in and out on the road again, the first interesting thing we saw was the swarm of Portuguese school children marching off down the road. We quickly leave Arzúa and follow the path through another forest. As we've left later in the morning than previous days, torches are not really needed. It's surprisingly warm, and I take off the fleece I'm wearing much earlier than I expected. My legs feel good, and although my feet feel quite battered, being able to see the kilometres countdown keeps us moving and motivated. We didn't see much of interest along the way, either that or we were just super focussed and didn't notice anything.

We arrive at 'O Pedrouzo' at 11:50. It's a tiny place with no shops and just one bar, where we stop off for a sandwich and a beer. Now with just 14kms until Monte do Gozo, it's all starting to come to an end. I feel both happiness and sadness.

We set off following more forest trails that occasionally open up alongside vast areas of farmland. Thanks to the stone markers now indicating which province we are in, we notice that we have left Lugo and entered the region of Santiago! After some kilometres, we arrive at the edge of the forest, and we see, hear and smell a motorway. We haven't seen cars moving this fast in over a week. We turn left, down the hill and follow a wide gravel path along a wire fence which separates us from the motorway. All the way down the hill, people have left hundreds, possibly thousands of simple crosses made from sticks and placed them in the holes of the fence.

Further down the path we smell another familiar and modern smell; aviation fuel and we realise that we're now steadily approaching Santiago airport. We feel good, like we're arriving but little did we know that we still have another 10kms of walking until we reach our albergue for the day in Monte do Gozo. These were definitely our hardest kilometres of the whole Camino. The stone markers are no longer indicating the remaining distance so we are left guessing. We climb and descend many hills, all on asphalt. The weather is cloudy, warm and humid, and we're feeling tired.

After seven more kilometres and another long road climb, we finally see a sign indicating an albergue! We are told this is the largest one of the whole Camino with about 800 beds in total, thankfully this is the sign indicating us to our destined accommodation for the night. As we approach, we see more and more people, walking around in flip-flops and without bags. This is a good sign as it shows that we're almost there. There is a large grass mound out to our left with a huge metal monument on top. You can tell there will be good views on the other side but we're too tired to go and have a look right now.

We arrive at the albergue at about 16:30 and we move into a room with four bunk beds. I have a hot shower and lie down for an hour. Seriously, I don't think I've ever felt this tired before in my life. Over 215kms of walking in eight days, is an average of almost 27kms everyday without any rest days, it has been intense.

After all the kilometres we've walked in the past week, and today being the longest of them all at 34kms, it feels great to think that we only have 5kms left to walk until we reach the cathedral of Santiago de Compostela.

We go for a walk around the complex of the albergue to help stretch our legs a bit and also to look for a place where we can eat later. We return to the large grass mound and its monument we passed earlier to go and see the impressive views. It is

19:45, and the falling sun is casting a beautiful golden light over the whole hill.

We found a regular place to have dinner. Afterwards, we hear a music concert out in the distance. Usually we would have gone to check it out, but instead we head back to the albergue to get some rest, so we have more energy for Santiago de Compostela in the morning.

Day Nine:

Monte do Gozo to Santiago de Compostela

Distance to Santiago: **5kms**

Stage Length: **5kms**

Santiago de Compostela Cathedral.

We wake up late for us at 07:30 and leave at about 08:15 after enjoying a very relaxing lie-in. On the walk down the road from Monte de Gozo there is again no need for torches as there is now plenty of daylight and as the day is beginning we see a spectacular sight. The entire valley below us is filled with a dense fog, and the buildings and trees on the top of the distant mountain are still visible, which creates an illusion where they appear to be floating on top of a cloud, it's a strange sight!

As we continue down the hill, we see various monuments dedicated to the Apostle Santiago. By about 09:00 we are clearly entering the city. We are walking through the outskirts, past many small shops and bars that are just starting to open for the day's business.

These signs in the city indicating the route to Santiago's cathedral are not as clear as we've been used to, maybe due to the maze of narrow streets or maybe we're just tired and distracted by this new world around us. As we enter the 'old town', we walk past several churches and buildings that have clearly been there for many centuries.

All of the buildings and streets in this area seem very well preserved, and I can imagine that visually not much has really changed in the last few hundred years. Following the narrow and winding path through the centre of the city, we walk through a small plaza that opens up the view above us. To our left and towering high above us, we see the enormous dominating spires of the city's cathedral and our final destination, scraping the sky above.

Continuing we once again see the view above us open up but this time we are now entering Plaza da la Quintana, the central plaza of the cathedral. We are approaching the plaza from behind the cathedral and to ensure that our first look will be the best, we resist turning around until we reach the far end. It would be a majestic sight on any typical day, but as we haven't seen a building this big or impressive in over a week, it is even more incredible. We finally get to see this building in all its glory with its signature double staircase leading up to the entrance. We stand there quietly, thinking about our journey up until this point.

We have arrived!

After some minutes, we walked to the top of this iconic staircase. We stop and look back at the plaza from above, and it slowly starts to sink in.

Still with our bags on we enter the cathedral. Thankfully we're not the only ones wandering around like this. At the far end we see the dramatic gilded gold altar area. We walk closer and see people queuing for the customary embracing of the Apostle Santiago, we join the queue fresh from the Camino and backpacks still attached. After a few long minutes of waiting, we turn and pass through a narrow stone doorway. Up some stairs and through a small passageway and we find ourselves up in the main altar area, within the far wall of the cathedral. We're in a small room above the cathedral floor; in it is a life-size gilded statue of the Apostle Santiago who is looking out through a window into the cathedral. I step on to the raised platform and give him the customary hug thanking him for our safe journey. We leave the room through the opposite side, down the stairs and through another narrow passageway, mirroring the first. But instead of walking out into the main floor of the cathedral, we continue down some more narrow stairs, underground this time into another small dimly lit room. We're now underneath the altar area. To our left there is a little cordoned off passageway where we see a small silver casket at the end, and we realise we're in the Apostle's crypt. This casket apparently contains the bones of the Apostle Santiago. Some of the people who enter the room, as soon as they see the chest immediately drop down to their knees, 'cross themselves' and start praying. It's a strange sight. I stay inside for a while longer to take in the surroundings. A minute later, I head out of the opposite side, up the stairs and back into the main area of the cathedral.

We leave the cathedral and once in the street, we ask for directions to the Pilgrim's Office where we can request our final stamp showing our arrival, and for the 'Compostela', the official certificate to confirm the completion of our journey. On arrival, we see a lot of people just hanging around casually outside. We go in and join the first queue leading upstairs. Once there, we then wait in a second queue until we are called forward.

Once called, I hand the girl my 'Credencial' (or 'pilgrim's passport') containing all the stamps I've collected along the way and therefore proving my journey. She then examines it, carefully checking the stamps and dates and asks me my motivation for walking the Camino. I need to answer either "religious", "religious and other" or "other". In the case of "religious" or "religious and other" the

Compostela is written in Latin. In the case of "other", there is a 'simpler' certificate written in Spanish.

She tells me that "the church officially recognises my arrival into Santiago de Compostela via the pilgrimage of Camino de Santiago", scribes my name in Latin onto the Compostela and presents it to me.

Still with our bags on, we walk around the city looking for a place to stay for the night, which we manage to find easily. We check into a hostel, and the kind lady shows us to what she describes as being the best room in the house, and nice it is too. It's big, very clean and has lots of natural light thanks to a large floor to ceiling window overlooking the street. We leave our things in the room and head out for a look around and to search for a good place to eat lunch.

We find a restaurant, sit outside and order a meat and potato omelette with seafood croquettes. The portions are enormous, and we can barely see the table for all the plates. The food is all homemade and tastes great, it is a welcome change to what we've been used to up until now. We are so hungry and have no problems finishing everything off. We continue exploring the city, getting used to our new surroundings. After some hours we returned to our hostel to catch up on some rest.

We leave the hostel again in the early evening to walk around the old town. It's a beautiful city, and the atmosphere here is unique. You can feel the deep-rooted history of the city all around us.

We choose a seafood restaurant to have dinner and after we return once again to the main plaza where we initially arrived earlier in the day. Here we stand watching a group of entertaining musicians in traditional dress, playing traditional Spanish songs on traditional instruments all with the cathedral in the background. Spectacular! Our journey on El Camino de Santiago has come to an end.

Final Thoughts

Now that I'm back home, fully recovered and rested, what are my thoughts on El Camino de Santiago? Did it live up to my expectations? Would I do it again?

Regardless of your reason for taking part in the adventure that El Camino de Santiago easily provides, it is a fantastic experience and one that will live with us for a very long time.

Being removed from our typical chaotic day-to-day routine, I found a liberating independence. We were living a relatively simple existence with our main focus on merely walking from A to B.

A lot of the time we were walking through deep countryside, albeit on a predetermined trail and I believe spending days on end amongst nature is quite a rare experience for most of us these days and certainly something that we appreciated.

I remember that we were a bit taken aback towards the end when we approached the motorway full of speeding cars, and then past the airport each filling our new environment with calm-destroying sounds and smells. This was something that we weren't used to and hadn't experienced in over a week!

Starting the day with sore feet and stiff legs is something we had to get used to, but I have to admit that I do like that aching muscle feeling the day after a heavy exercise session, I find it kind of rewarding. But as the days went on, the sore feet and stiff legs did start to recover quicker and feel better than on the previous day.

On one occasion, I developed an excruciating pain in my lower right back on every step. This was probably due to the day before, in a moment of tired thinking I decided it was going to be a good idea to (carefully) cut the skin off of two blisters on my foot. Needless to say they hadn't dried up by the next morning and it was like walking on hot coals the whole day. This no doubt had an effect on how I was walking and after a few thousand steps of walking strangely it took its effect in my lower back. Just goes to show how some bad decisions can escalate quickly.

Many of these 'injuries' need to be and can be tackled in the mind with positive thinking. As long as you look after yourself during and after the day's walk, making a habit of stretching your legs and body, cleaning and treating any injuries where needs be and applying necessary protection from the elements, you should have no problem in getting through it.

When you are enjoying pain-free walking, you are occupied physically, but mentally I found I had a lot of time to think about things, to let your mind wander and find clarity in thoughts and ideas, in both El Camino de Santiago and beyond.

Setting personal goals and getting out there to achieve them is a big part of completing El Camino. Both Bea and myself are naturally active people, but towards the end on one occasion after walking six or seven days in a row I found myself feeling more tired and exhausted than I had ever felt in my life (with the exception of when I was mountain biking through Peru). Saying that, it was nothing some wholesome food, a good rest and the curiosity of wanting to know what the next day brings couldn't sort out.

For anyone that enjoys adventure, finding and pushing themselves to new limits, accepting the unexpected and meeting people from all over the world, then taking part in El Camino de Santiago is an experience that I highly recommended. I learnt a lot from it, and I have wholly positive memories from it.

Due to our work schedule, we were only able to dedicate nine days to walking, in which we walked on average over 24kms per day. I like to think and hope that if the opportunity arises in the future, I would like to walk the full length of 'el Camino Francés'. Starting in St Jean Pied de Port in the French Pyrenees which is approximately 800kms from Santiago de Compostela and would take about five weeks to complete.

All the days before Sarria (which is 114kms from Santiago) had a nice calm atmosphere about them and all of the trails were relatively quiet. It was these days that I enjoyed the most. After Sarria it became much more crowded with all of the people racing to arrive to the next albergue, usually at about 12:30-13:00, to secure their place for the night and due to the amount of pilgrims, they generally fill up quickly.

If we were planning to extend our journey time to say an additional two to three weeks, then I don't believe it would be realistic to maintain our intensity. Instead for sure we would be scheduling in some rest days and shorter distances per day, making sure we don't burn ourselves out.

As with all things in life though, plans are bound to change, having reasonable knowledge about the route ahead helped us to adapt to changes in the plan.

We saw some couples walking with their young children who were either being pushed along in an all-terrain buggy or being carried in a harness on Dad's back. The additional planning and responsibility for this must be on another level. On the other hand I believe that with the right family it could be such a valuable and rewarding experience for both the child and parent. If doing this, I imagine a week or so would be the maximum time you would want to dedicate to it, and you could easily take full advantage, guilt-free, of any 'porta-baggage' service that you may find on-route. For accommodation it would be required to call ahead a day or two before to a private albergue to guarantee the needed beds, explaining that you are travelling with children. A private albergue would definitely be the way to go as Mum, Dad and a 3-year-old child sharing a room with 48 other people in a municipal albergue must be horrendous for everyone!

In the next chapter, you will find some additional first-hand tips and advice that I can share from my own experience. This information will hopefully provide interesting points for you to think about if you are considering or planning your own journey. I hope you find it useful.

Planning Tips, Advice and Useful Information

Training and Preparation

To help prepare ourselves physically and mentally during the weeks before we left we completed several 20-30km walks in the countryside, in an attempt to simulate the kind of terrain and distance that we were expecting. This provided essential feedback as it gave us an idea of what to expect and as to how we would be feeling at the end of each day. It also highlighted areas where we needed to make adjustments to our clothing, bag and other equipment.

Planning the Journey

Once we knew the number of days we had available to walk (including rest days if applicable), we could work out options for the total distance we could walk. Knowing this we were then able to check for towns on El Camino around this distance away from Santiago that would become our starting point.

From there on, we researched the route starting from this chosen location, we then found a good website detailing stage-by-stage information and printed off the relevant pages. This provided essential and detailed information including how to break the journey down into stages/days, the stage distance, the terrain (including elevation gain and drop), about the interesting towns and villages that we'd be passing through and about the albergues (hostels) that we would be staying in at the end of the day.

As opposed to taking a dedicated guidebook, we chose to carry printed A4 pages in a plastic document sleeve. This proved to be so much more convenient as it was lighter, it took up less space, and we could also discard any unneeded pages when necessary.

Albergues

The concept of the typical municipally run albergues seems kind of strange at first. They are all different, each with their own characteristics and their own pros and cons, but you soon realise that they are simply there to serve a purpose, to allow you to get cleaned up after a day of walking, and to provide you a clean bed for the night. They are all based in or on the outskirts of a small town or village, so finding food is usually only a short walk away. Typically a hearty three-course meal, specially prepared for people travelling on El Camino costs around 10€.

The public albergues are strictly first-come-first served, walkers take priority over cyclists and each one in our experience was clean and well maintained. Typically on arrival, you need to show your stamped 'Credencial' or 'Pilgrim's Passport', as only with this are you able to stay the night. Here you pay the nominal amount of about 7-10€ for the night's accommodation, they put a new stamp in your Credential and provide you with a clean mattress cover and a pillow. The public albergues cannot be booked in advance.

Each bedroom had between 4-50 beds in one room, and the bathrooms and showers were for male and female, but are all open and shared. In comparison a privately run albergue is more likely able to offer you your own room, a private shower and bathroom and it may have a more 'homely' feel about it, this would come at the cost of about 15-25€ per night.

Many of the albergues had a kitchen where you could prepare food, but most people choose to eat out in the town or village. If you decided to prepare food at the albergue, you would need to go out and buy the food or ingredients, return to the albergue, prepare it and then clean-up afterwards, but after a long day of walking, we found it was the last thing we wanted to do.

Most albergues either had a provided service for washing clothes, or they had their own washing machines for use, so we were able to give all our clothes a proper clean (as opposed to hand-washing) every now and then. Expecting this, and to get us started we took a small bag of washing powder with us, it didn't weigh much and took up almost no space. Alternatively, there were also dispensers selling small boxes of detergent.

As most albergues are based in or on the outskirts of a local community, the community does tend to supply for the needs of the pilgrims. You should easily be able to find restaurants, shops, supermarkets and pharmacies where you will be able to pick up food and needed supplies.

We had no problems charging our phones up in the albergues. If you're not lucky enough to have a charging point by your bed, (which you probably won't) you'll need to search out an available power point before bedtime and sit with your device or devices while they are charging.

Regarding Wi-Fi, it is becoming increasingly easier in some of the albergues to find access points to the internet be it free or paid, but if not, you should be able to find a place to connect from somewhere within the village.

Credencial Del Peregrino (Pilgrim's Passport)

One essential item you will need is an official 'Pilgrim's Passport' or a 'Credencial del Peregrino' as it's called in Spanish. This is what you use to officially identify that you are walking El Camino. You collect different identifying stamps from the numerous restaurants, churches, tourist offices (in larger towns) and the albergues that you stay in along the way, and it builds up to be a record of your route, certifying that you have been to these places. Without this document, you are not able to sleep in any of the public albergues, nor would you receive the certificate at the end in Santiago.

An official 'Credencial del Peregrino' can be obtained from a parish church, confraternity, Association of Friends of the Way of St. James, or any Christian institution related to the pilgrimage. Alternatively, an internet search for 'el camino de santiago pilgrim passport' can provide up-to-date information of where you can order one from in your region.

You have to stamp the 'credencial' at least twice a day on the last 100 km for pilgrims on foot or on horseback (or on the last 200km for those cycling).

The official considerations for the 'Credencial' are stated as below:

- The Credencial ('Pilgrim's Passport') is only for pilgrims on foot, bicycle or horseback, who wish to make the pilgrimage with a Christian sentiment, even if it is only with an attitude of search. The Credencial has the purpose of identifying the pilgrim; which is why the institution that issues it must be a parish church, confraternity, dioceses, Association of Friends of the Way of St. James, or any Christian institution related to the pilgrimage. The Credencial does not generate any rights to the pilgrim. It has two practical purposes: 1) access to hostels offered by the Christian hospitality of the way, 2) serve as certification in applying for the "Compostela" at the Cathedral of Santiago, which certifies you have made the pilgrimage.

- The "Compostela" accreditation (Certificate) is only granted to those who make the pilgrimage with Christian sentiment: "devotionis affectu, voti vel pietatis causa" (motivated by devotion, vote or mercy). And it is only granted to those who make the pilgrimage to reach the Tomb of the Apostle, doing in full at least the last 100 kilometres on foot or horseback, or the last 200 km by bike or 100 miles and the last km on foot.

- Therefore, the pilgrim's Credencial can only be issued by the Church through its institutions (Bishopric, Parish, Confraternity, etc. or, in any case, through institutions that are authorised by the Church).

- Hostels that receive no subsidies must be maintained, within austerity, with contributions from pilgrims (cleaning, looking after facilities, facilitating rest, financial aid…).

- Groups organised with a support car or by bicycle are requested to seek alternative shelter to the pilgrim hostels.

- The bearer of this Credencial accepts these conditions.

Safety

Everybody we met along the way was friendly, and we never had any feeling of being in danger. To the people in the villages, you are just another pilgrim passing through. We never encountered any dangerous animals, just a few fields of docile cows.

There has been some sad news in the last few years following the disappearance of a female walker who was travelling alone. Unfortunately, these kinds of incidents can happen anywhere and especially if travelling alone extra precautions are advised. Many people who set out walking alone, if they choose, find that they're not alone for very long as it is easy to meet other pilgrims. As you're all generally walking at the same pace and in the same direction, it is easy to become part of a group, if you choose.

When travelling on El Camino de Santiago, you will often find yourself in some very rural and remote parts of the Spanish countryside. However, after asking and searching around, it is widely accepted that yes, it is very safe to take part in the journey even if travelling alone.

What to Take

In this section, I offer my thoughts and opinions on some of the equipment that we took with us as well as some that we didn't.

Essential Equipment

My bag was a fairly basic 60 litre sized trekking one. It opened at the top, had some side pockets and had a comfortable waist strap, which is where most of the bag's weight should be supported from and not on the shoulders. Quite often it was only filled to about 80% of its full capacity, but the additional available space came in very useful for carrying daily food supplies etc. It's always better to have a bag that's a bit too big rather than a bit too small.

One essential item we took was a waterproof bag cover each, correctly sized for the bags we had. Quite often we found ourselves in wide-open countryside for hours on end that offered no protection at all from the elements. Imagine walking for several hours through heavy rain, the last thing you want is to arrive at the albergue to find out the rain has made its way through your bag and saturated your clothing and belongings. Without the bag cover even the bag itself may not be fully dry by the next morning.

We took a reasonably compact summer sleeping bag each and found it to be a perfect compromise. As we were always sleeping indoors, the temperature never became uncomfortably cold. My 'XL' sleeping bag measured up to be about 270mm x 130mm (10.5" x 5") and 750g (1lb 11oz). For the extra warmth and comfort a sleeping bag can provide, I would definitely retake one.

I would also recommend taking a pillowcase to use on the pillows provided by the albergues.

A smartphone can serve so many purposes in a single package. Providing you have sufficient battery life available, having access to a telephone, the internet, specific applications, alarm clock, camera, notepad, calculator, music etc. can all make a huge difference. To preserve as much battery as possible consider keeping the phone in a 'battery save' mode all of the time you are walking or at least turn off the WiFi and or the cellular function. You can't always guarantee that you'll be able to fully charge it each day, so battery preservation is a priority.

We took a couple of small, reasonably powerful LED waterproof torches which were invaluable on so many occasions. For example getting into and out of bed in the dark, packing your bag in the dark, early morning starts through the forest, walking on the road in the dark, through thick fog were some real-life examples of how we used them. One of them was more powerful at 180 lumens and 160mm (6.3") in length and one more compact one at 75 lumens and 93mm (3.66") in length.

A Swiss Army penknife also came in very useful on so many occasions, from having access to a knife, scissors, bottle and can openers, tweezers, a pin etc. It was something I kept close to hand and due to this it was extremely useful.

Having immediate access to clean drinking water is also something important to consider. I wish I had invested in a good quality 1-litre water bottle or two, instead carrying around a plastic bottle of water bought from the supermarket. As well as being known to release dangerous chemicals into the water, especially when exposed to sun, they can be a hive for bacteria and cannot be washed well. If you decide to use a good quality bottle, consider one you can clip to the outside of your bag if needs be, freeing up internal volume and providing easy access to water. There are generally places you can fill them up along the way, and I think that a 1-litre bottle per person would be adequate.

Earplugs are something simple and small, but they mustn't be overlooked and forgotten, that is if you value a reasonably quiet night's sleep! For the nights that we slept in a municipal albergue, about 70% of those were shared with heavy snorers. After a while, in the dark you start to hear people from around the room demanding silence by sending out a sharp and abrupt "SHhhhhh!!" hoping it will startle the accused enough to turn over and stop snoring. Also people stumbling around in the dark can be enough to break your sleep. Thankfully the majority of these disruptions can be prevented with earplugs. Pack a few spare pairs in your toiletry bag, you'll be happy you did!

Clothing

We tried to keep our cotton clothing to a minimum as wet cotton clothing can take hours to dry. Clothing can become extremely wet from sweat, after walking all day in hot weather, from a heavy downpour of rain and also from being washed. Ideally you don't want your clothing to take hours to dry, not to mention that wearing wet clothing will become uncomfortable quickly.

For footwear we both bought a new pair of walking shoes a few months before starting El Camino. We made sure that we used these shoes on several 15-25km practice walks to allow our feet to get used to the shoes, the shoes to form to our feet and for the leather and rubber to break in and loosen up in the right places. Thanks to this we knew our shoes were going to be comfortable on day one.

In addition to walking shoes, we also packed a pair of trekking sandals which proved to be invaluable on so many occasions. After wearing walking shoes all day, putting sandals on after having arrived at the albergue was one of our top priorities. Being able to walk around and expose our feet to air helped them to feel fresher and to recover far quicker than being stuffed into socks and tied up in a closed shoe. We even chose to wear them for parts of some stages for the same reasons. They also provide more support and protection than 'flip-flop' type sandals. They were also very useful for when showering to prevent getting any or passing on any foot infections.

I took a multi-functional Buff 'neck sleeve', which was used daily. It can be worn around the neck to keep the chills out, on hot days I would soak it in cold water, put it on around my neck and it provided instant cooling. Also, as a face warmer, lightweight hat, sweatband, it can keep UV rays off your skin, essential.

A full-brimmed hat is also highly recommended, it helps to keep the sun off your head, face and neck, to keep the rain and wind out of your eyes and provide a bit of warmth on chilly mornings.

Medical Bag

One of the responsibilities of being self-sufficient on El Camino is being able to administer basic first aid either to yourself, any companions or perhaps even help a fellow pilgrim in need. You never know when you might have to treat a small injury so a small bag of basic medical supplies, including plasters, sterilised wipes, blister patches, bandage, antihistamines, ibuprofen, pins etc. could make the difference between continuing or quitting.

Highly Recommended

If you're a keen reader (which if you're reading this you probably are), an ebook could be a worthwhile luxury to have, thanks to them being small, lightweight and having a reasonably long battery life. They also allow you to take a collection of books with you that you would like to read without adding additional weight or volume. You should find that you have several hours available during the afternoons to rest and a book is a welcome release from the day-to-day routine. Alternatively if you take a paper book with you, you may find that in the albergues you have the option to do a book exchange with your fellow pilgrims.

We took a small bag of washing powder for washing clothes and 4-metres of thin paracord to act as a travel clothesline. Using these we ended up washing our clothes by hand, bit-by-bit every day or two. Sometimes we could hang clothes up outside the albergue, sometimes you can find a place inside. Some albergues don't allow residents to dry their clothes in the bedroom, instead providing a separate undercover area for this, but they're not often fully dry in the morning, a big motivation to keep cotton clothing to a minimum!

One 'luxury' I took was the small packable travel hammock. At the end of a long day, having the opportunity to carefully set this up between trees and just lay there, swaying in the breeze was nothing short of pure bliss.

Things to Leave Behind

I would definitely recommend leaving all excessive and expensive electrical devices at home. Items such as iPads/tablets, DSLR cameras, GPS, speakers etc. I never felt that I needed, nor did I miss them at all. In fact, I was very happy not to have the responsibility of them nor having to carry them around, together with all their respective chargers and accessories. I was pleased I didn't have to worry about them getting wet when it rained continuously or about keeping them charged up, and

I didn't have to worry about them attracting attention and possibly being stolen when occasionally left unattended.

I never felt that I needed a dedicated GPS as the paths are so well marked. It may be a useful backup if things go very wrong. I did take one but in my experience, I had no real need to use it daily, it just became a device that I had to look after and keep charged up.

Many people used a pair of hiking poles to walk with, we didn't, and I have no regrets. I tried a pair for a short while and found them cumbersome and restrictive in that you can't use your hands for other things. Even the single wooden sticks that you can buy readily in many shops along the way, I felt offered no real benefit, I guess it comes down to personal preference, but we had no interest in using them.

I found zero need to carry cooking equipment (stoves, pans, cutlery etc.) as the route itself passes through so many small towns and villages where you can easily find plenty of restaurants, bakeries and the occasional small supermarket for any urgent missing supplies.

Recommended Pack-List

Have you ever wondered what's inside a typical pilgrim's bag? Would you like to compare your list with someone else's? If so, you can see my suggested list of things to take here.

Documents

- Passport / personal identification
- Credencial (Pilgrim's Passport)
- Travel medical insurance documents/European Health Insurance Card
- Printed information for your route

Essential Equipment

- Main Bag / Rucksack (60-80 litres – you don't need to fill it to the brim)

- Waterproof bag cover (for your size of bag)

- Sleeping sack or bag

- Pillowcase

- Smartphone and charger

- European 2 pin travel adapter, if required

- A Swiss Army knife

- Waterproof LED torch

- Water bottle (minimum 1 litre per person)

- Earplugs, several pairs

- Pen and paper

Clothing (non-cotton recommended)

- Walking shoes or boots
- Trekking sandals
- 4 pairs of socks
- 1-2 pairs of trousers
- 1-2 pairs of shorts
- 3-4 pairs of underwear
- 2-3 t-shirts
- 1 merino base layer and/or a lightweight fleece
- Jacket, lightweight and waterproof
- Buff / bandana
- Full brimmed hat
- Quick drying towel

Toiletries

- Shaving gear
- Toothbrush and toothpaste
- Sunscreen
- Shower gel and shampoo (all in one better)
- Nail clippers
- Foot cream or Vaseline
- Small packs of tissues
- Insect repellent

Medical Bag

- Ibuprofen tablets or other pain relief tablets
- Blister treatment patches
- Plasters
- Sterilising wipes
- Bandage
- Antihistamines
- Pins

Highly Recommended

- Laundry soap or powder

- Travel washing line or 4 metres of thin paracord

- Needle and thread

- Small roll of duct tape (useful for emergency repairs)

- Book / ebook

- Portable travel hammock

- Earphones

- Breakfast for the next day

- Snacks (energy bars, sweets etc)

Author Biography

Simon Green was born in the South-West of England and has lived in various locations around the world whilst studying, working as a graphic designer, teaching English and Fraud Prevention. Now, Simon lives in Spain, with his partner Bea and their 5-year-old son, Jack.

Simon has recently completed his first book, 'El Camino de Santiago: A 1st Hand View of Walking 220kms in 9 Days Across the North of Spain', which was inspired by his own journey across the famous pilgrim's route, and aims to share his experiences and knowledge with others.

When he has time to himself, Simon loves nothing better than keeping fit and especially cycling. He owns 7 bicycles and rides every day. He also likes to travel when he gets the chance, once taking an epic 500km trip through Peru on a bike and meeting some amazing people along the way.

You can contact Simon at:

Facebook – facebook.com/220kms.in.9days/

X – @220kms_in_9days

email – 220kms.in.9days@gmail.com

Thank you!

Thank you for reading El Camino De Santiago, A 1st Hand View Of Walking 220 Kms In 9 Days Across The North Of Spain.

Please don't forget to leave a review on Amazon if you found it useful!

Many thanks :)

Manufactured by Amazon.ca
Acheson, AB

12890179R00069